This journal belongs to:

....

Date:

....

52 Weeks of Gratitude

A ONE-YEAR JOURNAL

TO REFLECT, PRAY, AND RECORD THANKFULNESS

Ink &
Willow

Contents

Introduction

When thou hast truly thanked the LORD for every blessing sent,

But little time will then remain for murmur or lament.

HANNAH MORE

T he feelings we experience day by day—anxiousness, contentment, anger, happiness—can be a product of our outlook rather than our circumstances. We all have the power to choose an attitude of gratitude.

Over the next fifty-two weeks, this journal will help you turn your thoughts toward recognizing the blessings God has poured into your life, even during difficult times. As you do so, you will experience greater joy and find inner strength.

This book is divided into four sections, each highlighting a sphere of life in which you can find much to be thankful for: your home, your community, your faith, and the beauty around you. Each week features a Bible verse, a reflection question to journal on, and an action prompt to help you develop the practice of being grateful. Finally, at the end, you'll find a twelve-month gratitude list, where you can begin the daily habit of recording one thing you're thankful for.

This year, resolve to make gratitude to God your first response when life threatens to overwhelm you. Observe how your heart changes when you focus on your blessings rather than your problems. And don't be surprised if others around you start catching some of that joy!

This is the true nature of home—it is the
place of Peace; the shelter, not only from injury,
but from all terror, doubt, and division.

JOHN RUSKIN

Home. What a rich word, so full of promise and hope, memories and dreams, but also pain and sorrow mixed with joy and laughter. First steps. First pets. Favorite meals. Celebrations. Lessons. Sickness. Hugs. Bills to pay. Cozy pajamas. Summer barbecues.

Whether you live in a microscopic apartment or a seven-bedroom barndominium (it's really a thing), all alone or crowded among family members and appendages, the adage about there being no place like home generally rings true. Your home is—or should be—the one place you can feel safe, nourished, rested, and free to be yourself.

With so many people around the world suffering because of homelessness or abject living conditions, we should never take for granted having a place we can call home. Even on your toughest day, if you can climb into your own bed with a full belly, not fearing the night, you have much to be grateful for.

Learning to see the smallest comforts as blessings to celebrate will bring much joy into your home...and life!

WEEK 1

▼▼▼▼▼▼▼▼▼

Rest

Come to me, all you who are weary and burdened,

and I will give you rest.

MATTHEW 11:28

The times when we are most tired often coincide with when we have the most on our plates. But when we are exhausted, we are not operating at our best. Even though it's difficult to section out the time during our busy days, it is in these moments that we need to relax, refresh, and revitalize our spirits.

REFLECT

Do you feel guilty if you spend time resting instead of knocking items off your to-do list? How do you feel when you *don't* let yourself rest?

....

....

....

....

....

....

....

....
....
....
....
....
....
....
....
....
....
....
....
....
....
....
....
....
....
....
....
....

RESPOND

CARVE OUT—AHEAD OF TIME—
AT LEAST TEN MINUTES EACH
DAY THIS WEEK TO BE CALM
AND QUIET IN GOD'S PRESENCE
WITHOUT THINKING ABOUT
ANY OF YOUR RESPONSIBILITIES
OR CHORES. ASK GOD TO
GIVE YOU REST.

....
....
....

WEEK 2

▼▼▼▼▼▼▼▼▼

Nourishment

The people of Israel called the bread manna.
It was white like coriander seed and tasted
like wafers made with honey.

EXODUS 16:31

When the Israelites fled Egypt, they carried with them troves of food. Soon that abundance began to wane, and they called out to God for help. The manna He dropped from the sky provided all the vitamins, minerals, and nourishment the Israelites could ever need. Talk about the ultimate comfort food!

REFLECT

Think back to your favorite comfort food growing up. How did it make you feel whenever someone prepared it for you?

....

....

....

....

....

....

....

....

....

....

....

....

....

....

....

....

....

....

....

....

....

....

....

....

....

....

....

....

....

WEEK 3

▼▼▼▼▼▼▼▼▼

Hospitality

Share with the LORD's people who are in need.

Practice hospitality.

ROMANS 12:13

If being a hostess doesn't come naturally to you, it's tempting to leave hospitality to those who seem more naturally gifted in that area. However, opening our homes and lives to friends and strangers can be one of the most rewarding experiences we will ever have.

REFLECT

In what ways has God abundantly provided for your needs, either directly or through the generosity of others?

....

....

....

....

....

....

....

....

....
....
....
....
....
....
....
....
....
....
....
....
....
....
....
....
....
....
....

RESPOND

FIND SOMEONE IN YOUR CHURCH OR NEIGHBORHOOD WHO IS USUALLY ALONE AND INVITE HIM OR HER OVER FOR A MEAL, OR TAKE A HOME-COOKED DISH TO A PERSON OR FAMILY WHO MIGHT NEED THE EXTRA HELP.

WEEK 4

▼▼▼▼▼▼▼▼▼

Bath Time

*The L*ORD *blesses his people with peace.*

PSALM 29:11

A nice, warm bath can reduce stress and give you a sense
of calm and comfort. Enhance the atmosphere with fragrant
candles, bubbles, calming music, and maybe even a good
book. Afterwards, let all your worries swirl down the drain
while you wrap yourself in a nice, soft robe.

REFLECT

Think about the last time you soaked in a tub. How did it make
you feel?

....

....

....

....

....

....

....

....

....

....
....
....
....
....
....
....
....
....
....
....
....
....
....
....
....
....
....
....
....
....

RESPOND

CARVE OUT AT LEAST
HALF AN HOUR FOR
YOURSELF TO ENJOY
A BATH THIS WEEK,
AND USE THAT TIME
TO THANK GOD FOR HIS
GRACE AND BLESSINGS.

WEEK 5

▼▼▼▼▼▼▼▼▼

Water

Whoever drinks the water I give them will never thirst.

JOHN 4:14

Simply turn on a faucet, and you can access all the water you need. No wonder it's so easy to take it for granted! Yet if you've ever been on a long hike or bike ride where you ran out of water, you suddenly realize how important even a small amount is.

REFLECT

What are at least five ways water sustains and enriches your life?

....

....

....

....

....

....

....

....

....

....

....

....

....

....

....

....

....

....

....

....

....

....

....

....

....

....

....

....

....

....

....

....

....

RESPOND

THIS WEEK, KEEP A COUPLE
OF EXTRA WATER BOTTLES
IN YOUR CAR OR FRIDGE TO
SHARE WITH A HOMELESS
PERSON, SOMEONE WORKING
OUTSIDE, YOUR MAIL
CARRIER, OR SOMEONE ELSE
WHO MIGHT NEED IT OR
APPRECIATE IT.

▼▾▼▾▼▾▼▾▼

Returning Home

*By wisdom a house is built, and through understanding it
is established; through knowledge its rooms are filled with
rare and beautiful treasures.*

PROVERBS 24:3-4

After a long vacation, we begin to ache for the comforts of
home. There's something special about our homes. They give
us a sense of belonging that we can't find anywhere else.

REFLECT

Think of a time you were traveling and looked forward to
heading back home. What is it about home that makes you
long for it when you're not there?

....

....

....

....

....

....

....

▼▼▼▼▼▼▼▼▼

Laughter

[God] will yet fill your mouth with laughter

and your lips with shouts of joy.

JOB 8:21

You've heard it said that laughter is the best medicine. It's true! It boosts our moods, improves our immune systems, reduces anxiety, lowers blood pressure, and helps us connect in relationships.

REFLECT

What memories do you have of laughter in your home, either growing up or later in life? What made those moments special?

....

....

....

....

....

....

....

....

....

....

....

....

....

....

....

....

....

....

....

....

....

....

....

....

....

....

....

....

....

....

RESPOND

CHEER UP A FAMILY
MEMBER OR ROOMMATE
WHO HAS NOT LAUGHED IN
A WHILE BY TREATING HIM
OR HER TO AN ACTIVITY OR
EXPERIENCE YOU KNOW
HE OR SHE ENJOYS.

▼▼▼▼▼▼▼▼▼

Laundry Day

Therefore, as God's chosen people, holy and
dearly loved, clothe yourselves with compassion,
kindness, humility, gentleness, and patience.

COLOSSIANS 3:12

Washing, drying, folding, and putting away clothes is a chore many people dread. But consider the alternatives: not having clothing to launder, or not having access to facilities to wash them. Maybe these chores aren't so bad after all!

REFLECT

How can you be more grateful on laundry day?

....

....

....

....

....

....

....

....

....

....

....

....

....

....

....

....

....

....

....

....

....

....

....

....

....

....

....

....

....

RESPOND

THE NEXT TIME YOU DO
LAUNDRY, PRAY FOR EACH
FAMILY MEMBER AS YOU FOLD
HIS OR HER CLOTHES. IF YOU
LIVE ALONE, SAY A SHORT
PRAYER FOR DIFFERENT
PEOPLE IN YOUR CIRCLE FOR
EACH ITEM OF CLOTHING.

▼▼▼▼▼▼▼▼▼

Comfort

May your unfailing love be my comfort,

according to your promise to your servant.

PSALM 119:76

Comfort soothes our souls and allows us to be more relaxed and less stressed. Even just closing your eyes and picturing in your mind the things that bring you comfort can have a calming effect if you're feeling anxious.

REFLECT

When you've had a bad day, how does coming home make you feel better?

....

....

....

....

....

....

....

....

....

....

....

....

....

....

....

....

....

....

....

....

....

....

....

....

....

....

....

....

....

....

....

....

RESPOND

SIT ON OR WRAP
YOURSELF IN YOUR
FAVORITE COMFORTER
AND SPEND SOME TIME
THANKING GOD FOR
THE VARIOUS WAYS HE
COMFORTS YOU.

▼▼▼▼▼▼▼▼▼

Safety

The name of the LORD *is a fortified tower;*

the righteous run to it and are safe.

PROVERBS 18:10

Many factors influence our sense of safety. Whether it's financial, emotional, or physical, feeling safe is essential to our health and happiness.

REFLECT

What measures do you take to ensure your home is safe and secure? When is the last time you recognized God's protective hand?

....

....

....

....

....

....

....

....

....

....
....
....
....
....
....
....
....
....
....
....
....
....
....
....
....
....
....
....
....
....
....
....
....
....
....

RESPOND

TRY TO MAKE A HABIT
OF THANKING GOD FOR
WATCHING OVER YOUR
HOME WHENEVER YOU
LOCK YOUR DOOR.

▼▼▼▼▼▼▼▼▼

Therefore what God has joined together,

let no one separate.

MARK 10:9

Family can be one of our most important gifts, and it looks different for everyone. It could be our family of origin, the family we have created, or the communities around us.

REFLECT

Why is family unity so important, especially in the world we live in today?

....

....

....

....

....

....

....

....

....

....

....

....

....

....

....

....

....

....

....

....

....

....

....

....

....

....

....

....

....

....

....

....

....

....

RESPOND

THIS WEEK, MAKE A POINT OF EXPRESSING TO PEOPLE IN YOUR FAMILY HOW MUCH YOU APPRECIATE THEM AND FIND A WAY TO BLESS THEM IN RETURN. IF THEY LIVE WITH YOU, OFFER TO DO ONE OF THEIR CHORES TO GIVE THEM A BREAK.

WEEK 12

▼▼▼▼▼▼▼▼▼

Play

The city streets will be filled with

boys and girls playing there.

ZECHARIAH 8:5

Over the years, our responsibilities piled up and we stopped playing. Playtime is not just for kids though. It gives adults a chance to let down the walls, stimulate our imaginations, and improve our emotional well being. We all need to take some time to kick back and relax and play!

REFLECT

Think back to how you played as a child. What kinds of activities fed your curiosity, stretched your imagination, and inspired your creativity?

....

....

....

....

....

....

....

....

....

....

....

....

....

....

....

....

....

....

....

....

....

....

....

....

....

....

....

....

....

▼▼▼▼▼▼▼▼▼

Celebrate!

The meadows are covered with flocks and the valleys are

mantled with grain; they shout for joy and sing.

PSALM 65:13

Through celebration, we recognize when we, or people we love, have reached a goal, no matter how big or small. We honor the hard work in the midst of the mundane and in doing so lift our spirits.

REFLECT

What are some of the most memorable occasions you celebrated at home, either as a child or as an adult?

....

....

....

....

....

....

....

....

....
....
....
....
....
....
....
....
....
....
....
....
....
....
....
....
....
....
....
....
....
....
....
....
....
....

RESPOND

CREATE A LIFETIME OF
MEMORIES BY CARVING
OUT TIME ONCE A WEEK TO
CELEBRATE OR RECOGNIZE
SPECIAL MOMENTS IN YOUR
HOUSEHOLD, INSTEAD
OF WAITING FOR BIG
MILESTONES.

Community

We must learn to live together as brothers
or we will all perish together as fools.

MARTIN LUTHER KING JR.

In the beginning, God created a couple. A tiny family. Eventually, children came along and the family grew into a nation. Today, nearly 8 billion people live in 195 countries divided into provinces or states comprised of cities and towns further divided into neighborhoods or boroughs. Yet thousands of years after Adam and Eve walked in the Garden of Eden, the core of our communities remains the family unit.

In the traditional sense, families are made up of biologically related people, or those included through adoption or marriage. "Family" can also describe the people you worship with, neighbors who look out for and depend on one another, friends who live thousands of miles away but are readily available for one another, or the support system that sustains someone in distress.

Although social media promises to enhance our connections, we're seeing more and more loneliness, isolation, and depression. We desperately need *real* community. Not a few seconds of viewing and "liking" Facebook and Instagram posts, but eye contact, vulnerable conversations, meals around a table, hugs, long walks, board games, road trips, hospital visits, and Bible studies.

You need your people—and they need you.

These Little Ones

Come, my children, listen to me;
I will teach you the fear of the Lord.

PSALM 34:11

Whether you realize it or not, you are an influence to the children in your life. They experience the world through your actions, learn through your behaviors, and see the face of God through your love.

REFLECT

Think back to your childhood and the people who made you feel safe and loved. What did they do or say to make you feel that way?

....

....

....

....

....

....

....

....

....

....

....

....

....

....

....

....

....

....

....

....

....

....

....

....

....

....

....

....

....

....

....

RESPOND

WITHOUT RESORTING
TO BUYING GIFTS,
FIND A WAY TO "PAY
FORWARD" GOD'S
LOVE, WHICH YOU'VE
EXPERIENCED, TO A
CHILD IN YOUR FAMILY
OR COMMUNITY.

WEEK 15

▼▼▼▼▼▼▼▼▼

Wordsmiths

My heart is stirred by a noble theme as I recite my verses

for the king; my tongue is the pen of a skillful writer.

PSALM 45:1

Reading has benefits beyond increasing knowledge. A good book can offer insight into our anxieties or bring hope into a dark moment. At times, we may even find God whispering to us from the page, bringing our focus back to Him rather than what's in the world.

REFLECT

How have good books—fiction or otherwise—enriched your life?

....

....

....

....

....

....

....

....

....
....
....
....
....
....
....
....
....
....
....
....
....
....
....
....
....
....
....
....
....
....

RESPOND

TAKE TIME TO LEAVE
REVIEWS FOR AT LEAST
FIVE BOOKS YOU'VE
APPRECIATED, ESPECIALLY
ANY WHOSE AUTHORS
ARE NOT FAMOUS.
YOUR FEEDBACK WILL
ENCOURAGE THEM!

WEEK 16

▼▼▼▼▼▼▼▼▼

Teachers

I will instruct you and teach you in the way you should go;

I will counsel you with my loving eye on you.

PSALM 32:8

Besides educating us in the subjects we needed to learn, our teachers helped us grow and mature to become better versions of ourselves.

REFLECT

When you think back to your favorite teachers, what was it about them that had an impact on you?

....

....

....

....

....

....

....

....

....

THINK OF SOMEONE WHO
WOULD APPRECIATE AND
BENEFIT FROM COACHING
OR TUTORING FROM YOU
AND VOLUNTEER SOME
OF YOUR TIME TO HELP
HIM OR HER.

▼▼▼▼▼▼▼▼▼

Golden Agers

Gray hair is a crown of splendor;

it is attained in the way of righteousness.

PROVERBS 16:31

Older people can provide wisdom and advice from a lifetime of experience. They have endured things that the following generations will never witness. They bring history alive with the stories of their past. We have much to learn and appreciate about our elders.

REFLECT

Imagine the world without anyone over the age of 65. What would you miss the most?

....

....

....

....

....

....

....

....

··
··
··
··
··
··
··
··
··
··
··
··
··
··
··
··
··
··
··
··
··
··
··

RESPOND

CALL OR VISIT AN
ELDERLY PERSON THIS
WEEK. BEFORE ENDING
THE CONVERSATION,
ASK ABOUT THE BEST
ADVICE HE OR SHE
EVER RECEIVED.

▼▼▼▼▼▼▼▼▼

Workplace Connections

Let every person be quick to hear,

slow to speak, slow to anger.

JAMES 1:19 (ESV)

In many cases, you spend more waking hours with the people you work with than the people you live with. Therefore, it's important to foster valuable, positive relationships with your coworkers.

REFLECT

Think of past or present coworkers or employers who created a positive work environment through the way they communicated with others. What can you learn from their examples?

....

....

....

....

....

....

....

....

....
....
....
....
....
....
....
....
....
....
....
....
....
....
....
....
....
....
....
....
....
....
....

RESPOND

THIS WEEK, PRACTICE BEING A
GOOD LISTENER BY FOCUSING
INTENTLY WHEN COLLEAGUES
NEED YOUR ATTENTION. IF YOU
WORK ALONE, BE ATTENTIVE
DURING PHONE CALLS OR WITH
PEOPLE YOU ENCOUNTER
WHILE RUNNING ERRANDS.

▼▼▼▼▼▼▼▼▼

At Your Service

A generous person will prosper;

whoever refreshes others will be refreshed.

PROVERBS 11:25

Not all jobs are glamorous or even desirable, yet many of those jobs are essential to the well-being of society. We should be grateful for others who do the things we are either unwilling or unable to do.

REFLECT

Think of five types of jobs you've never had and would find too difficult to stick with. What would the world be like if no one else wanted to do those jobs?

....

....

....

....

....

....

....

....

WEEK 20

▼▼▼▼▼▼▼▼▼

Strangers

Do not forget to show hospitality to strangers,

for by so doing some people have shown hospitality

to angels without knowing it.

HEBREWS 13:2

If you are willing to risk rejection and start a conversation with someone you don't know, you might be surprised at how much brighter your world will be.

REFLECT

Think of a time a stranger helped you or a loved one. How did their kindness make a difference in your life?

....

....

....

....

....

....

....

....

....

....

....

....

....

....

....

....

....

....

....

....

....

....

....

....

....

....

RESPOND

....

THIS WEEK, PERFORM A
RANDOM ACT OF KINDNESS
FOR AT LEAST TWO
PEOPLE YOU DON'T KNOW,
WITHOUT EXPECTING
ANY RECOGNITION OR
SOMETHING IN RETURN.

....

....

....

....

WEEK 21

Neighbors

Better a neighbor nearby than a relative far away.

PROVERBS 27:10

Whether you live in an apartment complex, in a neighborhood of single-family homes, or out in the country miles away from your nearest neighbor, it's beneficial to be acquainted with those who are around you. Being welcoming creates a sense of positive energy, which leads to a happier community.

REFLECT

What are some things you appreciate about the people who live in your community?

....

....

....

....

....

....

....

....

....

....

....

....

....

....

....

....

....

....

....

....

....

....

....

....

....

....

....

....

....

....

RESPOND

REACH OUT TO AT
LEAST TWO NEIGHBORS
THIS WEEK, WHETHER
IT'S BY SIMPLY
INTRODUCING YOURSELF
OR BY OFFERING TO
HELP IN SOME WAY.

WEEK 22

▼▼▼▼▼▼▼▼▼

Diversity

There is neither Jew nor Gentile, neither
slave nor free, nor is there male and female,
for you are all one in Christ Jesus.

GALATIANS 3:28

Our world is colorful and beautiful, and our societies are becoming ever more diverse. We have the opportunity to understand and value different races, cultures, traditions, beliefs, and languages.

REFLECT

What are some things you appreciate about your friends or colleagues who are from cultures different from your own? What have you learned from them?

....

....

....

....

....

....

....

....

....
....
....
....
....
....
....
....
....
....
....
....
....
....
....
....
....
....
....
....
....
....
....

RESPOND

MAKE PLANS TO SPEND
TIME WITH SOMEONE YOU
NORMALLY WOULDN'T
HANG OUT WITH, PERHAPS
BECAUSE YOU'VE ASSUMED
YOU DON'T SHARE MUCH
IN COMMON.

▼▼▼▼▼▼▼▼▼

Healing Hands

When Jesus landed and saw a large crowd,
he had compassion on them and healed their sick.

MATTHEW 14:14

When you're sore, sick, depressed, or anxious, remember you are not alone. God sends people into our lives to heal, support, and comfort. Most times, they are just a phone call away.

REFLECT

How has God used health practitioners (doctors, dentists, counselors, massage therapists, and so on) to bring physical or emotional healing into your life?

....
....
....
....
....
....
....
....

....

....

....

....

....

....

....

....

....

....

....

....

....

....

....

....

....

....

....

....

....

....

....

RESPOND

THE NEXT TIME YOU
RECEIVE COMPASSIONATE
CARE THAT HELPS YOU
FEEL BETTER, SEND
A THANK-YOU CARD
EXPRESSING YOUR
APPRECIATION.

WEEK 24

▼▼▼▼▼▼▼▼▼

Mentors

Plans fail for lack of counsel, but with
many advisers they succeed.

PROVERBS 15:22

When you're in a new or challenging season, it's comforting to turn to someone who has "been there, done that." Mentors take you under their wings and guide you in both personal and professional situations.

REFLECT

Think of at least three people who have poured wisdom and knowledge into your life. What are some key lessons you gained from them that have shaped your life?

....

....

....

....

....

....

....

....

....

....

....

....

....

....

....

....

....

....

....

....

....

....

....

....

....

....

....

RESPOND

WRITE A NOTE OF THANKS
TO EACH OF THESE
PEOPLE, ACKNOWLEDGING
THE POSITIVE INFLUENCE
THEY HAVE HAD ON YOUR
LIFE. PRAY FOR THEM AND
THEN SEND THE NOTES.

WEEK 25

▼▾▼▼▾▼▼▾▼

Friends

Greater love has no one than this:

to lay down one's life for one's friends.

JOHN 15:13

Friends are there to laugh with, share life with, and pick us up when we're down.

REFLECT

What's the biggest sacrifice a friend has ever made for you and what did that act mean to you?

....

....

....

....

....

....

....

....

....

....

....

....

....

....

....

....

....

....

....

....

....

....

....

....

....

....

....

....

....

....

....

....

....

....

RESPOND

THINK OF A FRIEND GOING
THROUGH A ROUGH TIME. IN
A MANNER THAT SACRIFICES
YOUR OWN TIME, MONEY, OR
ENERGY, GO OUT OF YOUR
WAY TO HELP HIM OR HER IN
AN EXTRAVAGANT WAY.

▼▼▼▼▼▼▼▼▼

Fellowship

[Let us not give] up meeting together, as some are in the
habit of doing, but [encourage] one another.

HEBREWS 10:25

Spending time with other believers lifts us up and encourages
us to learn and grow in our faith. It also gives us a sense of
shared community, to remind us that we are not alone in this
world.

REFLECT

How does worshiping with other Christians encourage you in
your spiritual life? How do you feel when you've been apart
for a while?

....

....

....

....

....

....

....

....

....
....
....
....
....
....
....
....
....
....
....
....
....
....
....
....
....
....
....

Faith

Faith is not a refuge from reality. It is a demand

that we face reality, with all its difficulties,

opportunities, and implications.

EVELYN UNDERHILL

We talk about faith all the time, but it can be hard to explain and still harder to practice. How do we hold on to faith when we feel overwhelmed by political unrest, natural disasters, and stressful circumstances in our personal lives? Why should we continue to trust in a God we cannot see?

When we slow down long enough to recognize and count our blessings, to acknowledge how God has answered prayers—even prayers we forgot to utter—and to praise Him for His goodness and provision, our perspective shifts; and gratitude, followed by joy, begins to replace resentment, fear, and doubt.

Spiritual disciplines such as prayer, Bible study, worship, and fellowship pave the road ahead of us as we go through life. That road is not generally the popular one, but it's solid, steady, and often surprisingly breathtaking! Best of all, the "pioneer and perfecter of faith" (Hebrews 12:2) walks alongside us, and He's the best traveling companion we could ever have.

▼▼▼▼▼▼▼▼▼

Giving Thanks

And he took bread, gave thanks and broke it,
and gave it to them, saying, "This is my body given
for you; do this in remembrance of me."

LUKE 22:19

Thankfulness is acknowledging the goodness in our lives, and it connects us with something larger than ourselves.

REFLECT

If you knew you had only twelve hours to live, how would you spend that time and what would your attitude be like?

....

....

....

....

....

....

....

....

....

....

....

....

....

....

....

....

....

....

....

....

....

....

....

....

....

....

....

....

....

....

....

....

RESPOND

READ THROUGH LUKE 22 AND
MAKE NOTES OF ALL THE
CHOICES JESUS MADE ON
THE DAY HE KNEW HE WOULD
BE BETRAYED AND LED TO
HIS EXECUTION. ASK GOD
TO SHOW YOU HOW YOU CAN
DEMONSTRATE GRACE
LIKE JESUS DID.

Healing

One of them, when he saw he was healed,

came back, praising God in a loud voice.

He threw himself at Jesus' feet and thanked him.

LUKE 17:15–16

Sometimes when we are in the midst of illness, we become afraid or discouraged. In those times when it's difficult to have a positive outlook, we can still have a *hopeful* one. Whatever you are facing, remind yourself that you are not alone. God is right beside you.

REFLECT

Think back to times in your life when you were sick or in great pain. How did God help you get through those difficulties?

....

....

....

....

....

....

....

....

....
....
....
....
....
....
....
....
....
....
....
....
....
....
....
....
....
....
....
....
....
....

▼▼▼▼▼▼▼▼▼

Grace

The Lord is compassionate and gracious,

slow to anger, abounding in love.

PSALM 103:8

Grace is extending mercy to those who have harmed us, whether or not they "deserve it." Forgiving others does not excuse them from their behavior, but it allows us to move forward in our lives.

REFLECT

How does your experience of seeking forgiveness from God differ from your experience of seeking forgiveness from other people?

....

....

....

....

....

....

....

....

....
....
....
....
....
....
....
....
....
....
....
....
....
....
....
....
....
....
....
....
....

RESPOND

THINK OF SOMEONE TOWARD
WHOM YOU HAVE BEEN
HARBORING RESENTMENT
OR BITTERNESS. THIS WEEK,
MAKE A POINT OF PRAYING
FOR HIM OR HER AND
FINDING A WAY TO EXTEND
COMPASSION, GRACE,
AND LOVE.

▼▼▼▼▼▼▼▼▼

Consider it pure joy, my brothers and sisters, whenever
you face trials of many kinds, because you know that the
testing of your faith produces perseverance.

JAMES 1:2–3

It's easy to confuse joy with happiness. Happiness is a feeling that can be dependent on situations when things are going well, whereas joy is an emotion that runs deeper. Joy can remain in our souls, even in times of suffering.

REFLECT

Why is it hard to feel joyful when you're going through hard times? How can trusting in God restore your joy?

....

....

....

....

....

....

....

....

RESPOND

IN YOUR JOURNAL, USE
TWO COLUMNS TO KEEP A
RUNNING LIST OF THINGS YOU
FEEL ANXIOUS ABOUT AND
THINGS YOU FEEL GRATEFUL
FOR. OBSERVE HOW YOUR
SENSE OF JOY CHANGES
WHEN YOUR GRATITUDE
LIST IS LONGER.

▼▼▼▼▼▼▼▼▼

Prayer

Dear friends, if our hearts do not condemn us,

we have confidence before God and receive

from him anything we ask, because we keep his

commands and do what pleases him.

1 JOHN 3:21–22

Even when we can't seem to hear God, He is always listening. Pray in times of joy and in times of trouble. Pray for yourself as well as for others.

REFLECT

What specific prayers has God answered in your life recently? How do you feel about the way He answered them?

....

....

....

....

....

....

....

....

....

....

....

....

....

....

....

....

....

....

....

....

....

....

....

....

....

....

....

....

RESPOND

THINK OF ABOUT THIRTY
PEOPLE YOU WANT TO
REGULARLY PRAY FOR AND
ASSIGN EACH NAME ONE DAY
OF THE MONTH. IF YOU CAN,
SEND A QUICK MESSAGE ASKING
HOW YOU CAN PRAY FOR
THEM, OR LET THEM
KNOW THAT YOU DID
AFTERWARD.

▼▼▼▼▼▼▼▼▼

Truth

If you hold to my teaching, you are really
my disciples. Then you will know the truth,
and the truth will set you free.

JOHN 8:31–32

In today's technological age, the pursuit of truth is a challenging endeavor. We must tune our ears and feelings to truth, rather than get lost in the noise of never-ending information.

REFLECT

How have you pursued truth in your life? What difference has it made?

....

....

....

....

....

....

....

....

....

....

....

....

....

....

....

....

....

....

....

....

....

....

....

....

....

....

....

....

....

....

....

$RESPOND$

THANK GOD FOR
SPECIFIC TRUTHS THAT
HAVE HELPED YOU
EXPERIENCE FREEDOM,
AND ASK HIM TO GIVE
YOU THE COURAGE TO
SHARE THOSE TRUTHS
WITH OTHERS.

WEEK 33

▼▼▼▼▼▼▼▼▼

Hope

But those who hope in the Lord will renew their strength.

They will soar on wings like eagles; they will run and not

grow weary, they will walk and not be faint.

ISAIAH 40:31

Even in the most challenging times, keep hope in God. His love is unfailing and in Him we have a certain and secure future.

REFLECT

How is putting your hope in God different from putting it in other people or in your circumstances?

....

....

....

....

....

....

....

....

....

....

....

....

....

....

....

....

....

....

....

....

....

....

....

....

....

....

....

....

....

....

....

....

....

RESPOND

MEMORIZE ISAIAH 40:31
AND MAKE A POINT OF
MEDITATING ON IT FOR A
FEW MINUTES WHENEVER
YOU SET OUT FOR A
WALK OR RUN.

▼▼▼▼▼▼▼▼▼

Peace

I have told you these things, so that in me you may

have peace. In this world you will have trouble.

But take heart! I have overcome the world.

JOHN 16:33

It's tempting to wish for smooth sailing at all times, in all things. Even Jesus tells us that's not possible in this world. There will be bumps that can toss us in unexpected ways. True peace— divine peace—comes only through relationship with Him.

REFLECT

When do you feel most at peace? How do you hold on to that peace when life gets chaotic?

....

....

....

....

....

....

....

....

....

....

....

....

....

....

....

....

....

....

....

....

....

....

....

....

....

....

....

▼▼▼▼▼▼▼▼▼

Worship

Praise the Lord, *my soul;*

all my inmost being, praise his holy name.

PSALM 103:1

Worship is more than an outward expression of our devotion to God. It's praising Him with every part of ourselves—body, mind, and soul. When we put our full self into worship, then we are placing God as a top priority in our daily lives.

REFLECT

What would it look like if you praised God with all your "inmost being"?

....

....

....

....

....

....

....

....

....

....

....

....

....

....

....

....

....

....

....

....

....

....

....

....

....

....

....

....

....

....

....

....

....

....

....

....

....

RESPOND

FIND FIVE NEW WAYS
TO WORSHIP GOD
THIS WEEK, USING
DIFFERENT PARTS OF
YOUR BEING (SUCH AS
YOUR HANDS, VOICE,
FEET, AND SO ON).

▼▼▼▼▼▼▼▼▼

Courage

The LORD *himself goes before you and will be*

with you; he will never leave you nor forsake you.

Do not be afraid; do not be discouraged.

DEUTERONOMY 31:8

Being courageous doesn't mean being without fear. After all,
it's natural to feel anxious in response to a stressful situation.
Courage comes as a result of facing your fears and not letting
them take your heart captive.

REFLECT

Who has been a good example to you of trusting God during
uncertain times?

....

....

....

....

....

....

....

....

....

....

....

....

....

....

....

....

....

....

....

....

....

....

....

....

....

....

....

....

....

....

We love because he first loved us.

1 JOHN 4:19

God's love is unconditional. It isn't based on feelings—His *or* ours. It isn't based on how we act or what we do. God loves us because He *is* love.

REFLECT

How easy is it to believe that God loves you? How does your perception of God's love for you affect how you love others?

....

....

....

....

....

....

....

....

....

....

RESPOND

THINK OF THREE
PEOPLE WHO MIGHT BE
STRUGGLING TO BELIEVE
GOD LOVES THEM. TAKE
TIME THIS WEEK TO
REMIND AND REASSURE
THEM THAT HE DOES.

WEEK 38

▼▼▼▼▼▼▼▼▼

Cheerful Giving

Each of you should give what you have decided in your

heart to give, not reluctantly or under compulsion,

for God loves a cheerful giver.

2 CORINTHIANS 9:7

Are you a generous and cheerful giver? Giving expresses a heart of gratitude in passing along a portion of the blessings we have received.

REFLECT

How do you feel when you give someone a thoughtful and generous gift and they react with delight and appreciation?

....

....

....

....

....

....

....

....

....

....

....

....

....

....

....

....

....

....

....

....

....

....

....

....

....

....

....

....

....

....

....

....

....

....

RESPOND

DETERMINE IF SOMEONE HAS
AN URGENT NEED, WHETHER
IT BE A NEIGHBOR, CHURCH,
OR A NONPROFIT, AND
THEN FIND A WAY TO GIVE
EXTRAVAGANTLY, TRUSTING
GOD TO PROVIDE FOR
YOU AS YOU DO.

▼▼▼▼▼▼▼▼▼

Perseverance

We also glory in our sufferings, because we know
that suffering produces perseverance; perseverance,
character; and character, hope.

ROMANS 5:3–4

Perseverance is the ability to keep doing something despite difficulties, obstacles, or opposition. It's not an act of waiting until your circumstances change, it's about changing your mindset to keep moving forward.

REFLECT

Think of a time you didn't give up, even though it was hard to keep going. How did trusting God redeem the situation?

....

....

....

....

....

....

....

....

....

....

....

....

....

....

....

....

....

....

....

....

....

....

....

....

....

....

....

....

....

....

....

....

RESPOND

CHECK IN WITH A LOVED ONE
WHO FEELS DISCOURAGED
BECAUSE OF FAILURE,
REJECTION, OR SOME OTHER
HARDSHIP. OFFER TO PRAY
FOR HER AND THEN ASK
HOW YOU CAN HELP
HER PERSEVERE.

Beauty

Beauty

The pursuit of truth and beauty is a sphere of activity in

which we are permitted to remain children all our lives.

ALBERT EINSTEIN

How does one define "beauty" when it seems so subjective, when standards of beauty change more often than most of us change our bed sheets? Why is it that the idea of beauty—which is supposed to be something positive—causes so much anxiety, especially for women?

Perhaps we forget that beauty has little to do with physical attributes that can be measured and weighed. While we may assess the *health* of a tree or flower by observing its height or color, we certainly don't judge its *beauty*. We instinctively recognize that the same bumps and abnormalities that make plants and animals unique also make them beautiful.

We appreciate paintings, quilts, operas, architecture, ballet, and butterflies not because they are perfect products stamped out in a factory but because they are the result of love combined with creativity. In fact, the more authentic—or *truthful*—anything is about its nature, the more beautiful it is to the beholder, especially one who pursues truth and beauty as children do.

WEEK 40

▼▼▼▼▼▼▼▼

Seasons

As long as the earth endures, seedtime

and harvest, cold and heat, summer and winter,

day and night will never cease.

GENESIS 8:22

In the midst of the cold, dreary winter, it's hard to appreciate the white, flawless snow. And we aren't grateful for the rain and thunder until the heat overwhelms us. Be present in the season you are in because while they aren't the same everywhere, they are important to life.

REFLECT

Think of one beautiful thing you enjoy about each of the four seasons. What would the seasons be like without those things?

....

....

....

....

....

....

....

....

....

....

....

....

....

....

....

....

....

....

....

....

....

....

....

....

....

....

....

....

RESPOND

WRITE OUT FOUR SEPARATE
SENTENCE-PRAYERS THANKING
GOD SPECIFICALLY FOR THE
THINGS YOU ENJOY ABOUT
EACH SEASON. ATTACH EACH
ONE TO YOUR PLANNER WHERE
THE CORRESPONDING SEASON
STARTS, TO REMIND YOU
TO BE GRATEFUL.

▼▼▼▼▼▼▼▼

Trees

Then God said, "Let the land produce vegetation: seed-
bearing plants and trees on the land that bear fruit with
seed in it, according to their various kinds." And it was so.

GENESIS 1:11

Trees are a gift from God, and essential to our survival. They convert carbon dioxide into oxygen for us to breathe, they provide shelter for birds and animals, and so much more.

REFLECT

What are at least five other reasons to be grateful for trees?

....

....

....

....

....

....

....

....

....

....

....

....

....

....

....

....

....

....

....

....

....

....

....

....

....

....

....

....

....

....

....

....

....

....

▼▼▼▼▼▼▼▼▼

Inner Beauty

Your beauty should...be that of your inner self, the

unfading beauty of a gentle and quiet spirit,

which is of great worth in God's sight.

1 PETER 3:3–4

The idea of beauty causes so much anxiety, especially for women. Yet, obsessing about how you look prevents you from viewing yourself through the eyes of God.

REFLECT

Opinions about physical beauty vary widely. How is that different when it comes to inner beauty? Which is better to pursue?

....

....

....

....

....

....

....

....

....

....

....

....

....

....

....

....

....

....

....

....

....

....

....

....

....

....

....

....

....

....

....

THINK OF THREE PEOPLE YOU
ADMIRE FOR THEIR INNER
BEAUTY. THIS WEEK, WRITE
EACH A NOTE EXPRESSING
WHAT YOU APPRECIATE
ABOUT THEM.

▼▼▼▼▼▼▼▼

Light

God saw that the light was good, and he

separated the light from the darkness.

GENESIS 1:4

Having the right amount of light can make all the difference when you're walking late at night, working on a detailed project, or trying to create ambiance for a special occasion.

REFLECT

Can you imagine life without sunlight or any other source of light? How is light a gift from God?

....

....

....

....

....

....

....

....

....

WRITE OUT A PRAYER
THANKING GOD FOR SPECIFIC
WAYS LIGHT ADDS BEAUTY
TO YOUR LIFE.

WEEK 44

▼▼▼▼▼▼▼▼▼

Animals

The righteous care for the needs of their animals.

PROVERBS 12:10

There's a reason videos of kittens, baby goats, and elephants are so popular on the Internet. Their cuteness delights us, their mischievousness makes us laugh, and their intelligence astounds us.

REFLECT

Besides the companionship of pets, what are other ways animals are a blessing in your life (e.g. honey from bees and wool from sheep)?

....

....

....

....

....

....

....

....

....
....
....
....
....
....
....
....
....
....
....
....
....
....
....
....
....
....
....
....
....
....
....
....

RESPOND

THIS WEEK, BE MINDFUL
OF THE THINGS YOU
ENJOY BECAUSE GOD
CREATED ANIMALS
AND MAKE A POINT OF
THANKING HIM WHENEVER
YOU THINK OF ONE.

Music

My heart, O God, is steadfast, my heart is steadfast;
I will sing and make music.

PSALM 57:7

The people who make movies—and commercials—tweak and refine arrangements to get a certain type of emotional response. It can pull and tug at our hearts and sit with us for days. The music we choose to play or listen to matters because music inevitably pierces the depths of our souls.

REFLECT

Imagine a world without music of any kind. How would your life be different?

....

....

....

....

....

....

....

....

RESPOND

THINK OF SOMEONE
WHOSE MUSICAL TALENT
YOU APPRECIATE AND
AFFIRM HIM OR HER THIS
WEEK THROUGH A NOTE,
PHONE CALL, OR GIFT.

▼▼▼▼▼▼▼▼

Flowers

Consider how the wild flowers grow. They do not labor
or spin. Yet I tell you, not even Solomon in all his
splendor was dressed like one of these.

LUKE 12:27

"Stop and smell the roses" isn't just a clever way to say "slow down." It's good advice to take literally, too. Taking time to pause and marvel at the intricate beauty of flowers can speak to our hearts.

REFLECT

An estimated four million varieties of flowers exist around the world. What does that tell you about God's creativity? About His love for you?

....

....

....

....

....

....

....

....

....

....

....

....

....

....

....

....

....

....

....

....

....

....

....

....

....

....

....

....

....

RESPOND

TREAT YOURSELF
TO A BOUQUET OF
FLOWERS THIS WEEK
(OR A SINGLE BLOOM).
WHENEVER YOU SEE
IT, OFFER A PRAYER OF
THANKS TO GOD.

▼▼▼▼▼▼▼▼▼

Colors

Though your sins are like scarlet, they shall be

as white as snow; though they are red as

crimson, they shall be like wool.

ISAIAH 1:18

From the deep red of a pomegranate to the iridescent blue of a peacock feather to the sunny yellow of a dandelion, our world presents a feast of colors for our eyes.

REFLECT

What is your favorite color? How does it make you feel? What are some beautiful things God created in that color?

....

....

....

....

....

....

....

....

....

....

....

....

....

....

....

....

....

....

....

....

....

....

....

....

....

....

....

....

....

....

RESPOND

SURPRISE A FRIEND
THIS WEEK WITH A
LITTLE TREAT IN HER
FAVORITE COLOR AND
USE THE OCCASION TO
TELL HER HOW MUCH
YOU APPRECIATE HER.

▼▼▼▼▼▼▼▼▼

Taste and see that the LORD *is good; blessed is*

the one who takes refuge in him.

PSALM 34:8

There is a vast combination of flavors available for our palate to experience on a daily basis. Flavor brings zest to our taste buds and can be a blanket of comfort during difficult days.

REFLECT

Of the five basic tastes (sweet, sour, bitter, salty, and savory), which is your favorite? How enjoyable would eating be without this range of flavors?

....

....

....

....

....

....

....

....

....

....

....

....

....

....

....

....

....

....

....

....

....

....

....

....

....

....

....

....

....

....

....

....

RESPOND

THIS WEEK, WHENEVER YOU
THANK GOD FOR PROVIDING
NOURISHMENT THROUGH
THE FOOD YOU EAT, MAKE
A POINT OF THANKING HIM
FOR THE GIFT OF FLAVOR,
TOO. (AND EAT SLOWLY TO
ENJOY THOSE FLAVORS!)

WEEK 49

▾▾▾▾▾▾▾▾▾

Touch

Jesus had compassion on them and touched their eyes.

Immediately they received their sight and followed him.

MATTHEW 20:34

There's something wonderful about snuggling into your terry robe after a shower or squishing wet sand between your toes when you're at the beach. But nothing compares to the warm embrace of a loved one after a trying day or the gentle kiss of a child before bed.

REFLECT

Think of the various textures—both lovely and unpleasant— your fingers run across each day. How is human touch different? How has it been a gift in your life?

....

....

....

....

....

....

....

....

....

....

....

....

....

....

....

....

....

....

....

....

....

....

....

....

....

....

....

....

....

BE MINDFUL OF WHAT
MESSAGE YOUR TOUCH
SENDS TO THOSE YOU
ARE IN CONTACT WITH
THIS WEEK. FIND WAYS
TO OFFER A GENTLE AND
HEALING TOUCH TO
THOSE WHO NEED IT.

▼▼▼▼▼▼▼▼▼

Art

He has filled them with skill to do all kinds of work as

engravers, designers, embroiderers in blue, purple, and

scarlet yarn and fine linen, and weavers—all of them

skilled workers and designers.

EXODUS 35:35

If we limit our idea of art to things like paintings and
sculptures, we miss out on other dazzling artistry around us.
Your clothes, furniture, and even your dishes can become
more beautiful when you view them with different eyes.

REFLECT

Walk around your house and consider how many items were
designed with artistic talent. How does human creativity echo
the artistry in God's creation?

....

....

....

....

....

....

....

RESPOND

PLAN AN ART-RELATED
OUTING WITH YOUR
FAMILY OR A COUPLE OF
FRIENDS THIS MONTH,
SUCH AS VISITING A
MUSEUM OR JOINING A
PAINT NIGHT.

WEEK 51

▾▾▾▾▾▾▾▾▾

Fragrance

Perfume and incense bring joy to the heart,
and the pleasantness of a friend springs
from their heartfelt advice.

PROVERBS 27:9

Have you ever been transported back to another time and place just by a smell? Although invisible, smells—whether pleasant or nauseating—can elicit emotions and memories.

REFLECT

How do you react when you smell coffee? Lilacs? A loved one's familiar perfume? What are five scents you're grateful for today?

....

....

....

....

....

....

....

....

The Sky

The heavens declare the glory of God;

the skies proclaim the work of his hands.

PSALM 19:1

Sunsets, rainbows, lightning, fluffy white clouds, stars, and even a simple clear, blue sky...Have you ever noticed how much happens in the vast expanse over our heads?

REFLECT

What do the different ways the sky "proclaims" God's glory tell you about His nature?

....

....

....

....

....

....

....

....

....

....

TRY TO GRAB AT LEAST
FIVE MINUTES EACH DAY
THIS WEEK TO GAZE AT
THE SKY—PERHAPS AT
DIFFERENT TIMES OF THE
DAY—AND THANK GOD
FOR THE "WORK OF
HIS HANDS."

Daily

Gratitude

On the pages that follow, record one thing every day that you are thankful for—even if it's something small or simple. Whenever your spirits need a boost, read through the list you've created and remember the joy attached to each day's gratitude.

▼▼▼▼▼▼▼▼▼▼

January

1 ....

2 ....

3 ....

4 ....

5 ....

6 ....

7 ....

8 ....

9 ....

10 ....

11 ....

12 ....

13 ....

14 ....

15 ....

16 ....

17 ....

18 ....

19 ....

20 ....

21 ....

22 ....

23 ....

24 ....

25 ....

26 ....

27 ....

28 ....

29 ....

30 ....

31 ....

GRATITUDE

▼▼▼▼▼▼▼▼▼

February

1 ....
2 ....
3 ....
4 ....
5 ....
6 ....
7 ....
8 ....
9 ....
10 ....
11 ....
12 ....
13 ....
14 ....
15 ....
16 ....
17 ....
18 ....
19 ....
20 ....
21 ....
22 ....
23 ....
24 ....
25 ....
26 ....
27 ....
28 ....
29 ....

March

1 ....
2 ....
3 ....
4 ....
5 ....
6 ....
7 ....
8 ....
9 ....
10 ....
11 ....
12 ....
13 ....
14 ....
15 ....
16 ....
17 ....
18 ....
19 ....
20 ....
21 ....
22 ....
23 ....
24 ....
25 ....
26 ....
27 ....
28 ....
29 ....
30 ....
31 ....

GRATITUDE

▼▼▼▼▼▼▼▼▼

April

1 ....
2 ....
3 ....
4 ....
5 ....
6 ....
7 ....
8 ....
9 ....
10 ....
11 ....
12 ....
13 ....
14 ....
15 ....
16 ....
17 ....
18 ....
19 ....
20 ....
21 ....
22 ....
23 ....
24 ....
25 ....
26 ....
27 ....
28 ....
29 ....
30 ....

GRATITUDE
▾▾▾▾▾▾▾▾▾▾

May

1 ....

2 ....

3 ....

4 ....

5 ....

6 ....

7 ....

8 ....

9 ....

10 ....

11 ....

12 ....

13 ....

14 ....

15 ....

16 ....

17 ....

18 ....

19 ....

20 ....

21 ....

22 ....

23 ....

24 ....

25 ....

26 ....

27 ....

28 ....

29 ....

30 ....

31 ....

GRATITUDE

▾▾▾▾▾▾▾▾▾▾

June

1 ....
2 ....
3 ....
4 ....
5 ....
6 ....
7 ....
8 ....
9 ....
10 ....
11 ....
12 ....
13 ....
14 ....
15 ....
16 ....
17 ....
18 ....
19 ....
20 ....
21 ....
22 ....
23 ....
24 ....
25 ....
26 ....
27 ....
28 ....
29 ....
30 ....

GRATITUDE

▼▼▼▼▼▼▼▼▼

July

1 ....
2 ....
3 ....
4 ....
5 ....
6 ....
7 ....
8 ....
9 ....
10 ....
11 ....
12 ....
13 ....
14 ....
15 ....
16 ....
17 ....
18 ....
19 ....
20 ....
21 ....
22 ....
23 ....
24 ....
25 ....
26 ....
27 ....
28 ....
29 ....
30 ....
31 ....

GRATITUDE

▼▼▼▼▼▼▼▼▼▼

August

1 ....
2 ....
3 ....
4 ....
5 ....
6 ....
7 ....
8 ....
9 ....
10 ....
11 ....
12 ....
13 ....
14 ....
15 ....
16 ....
17 ....
18 ....
19 ....
20 ....
21 ....
22 ....
23 ....
24 ....
25 ....
26 ....
27 ....
28 ....
29 ....
30 ....
31 ....

GRATITUDE

▼▼▼▼▼▼▼▼▼▼

September

1 ....
2 ....
3 ....
4 ....
5 ....
6 ....
7 ....
8 ....
9 ....
10 ....
11 ....
12 ....
13 ....
14 ....
15 ....
16 ....
17 ....
18 ....
19 ....
20 ....
21 ....
22 ....
23 ....
24 ....
25 ....
26 ....
27 ....
28 ....
29 ....
30 ....

October

1 ....
2 ....
3 ....
4 ....
5 ....
6 ....
7 ....
8 ....
9 ....
10 ....
11 ....
12 ....
13 ....
14 ....
15 ....
16 ....
17 ....
18 ....
19 ....
20 ....
21 ....
22 ....
23 ....
24 ....
25 ....
26 ....
27 ....
28 ....
29 ....
30 ....
31 ....

GRATITUDE

▼▼▼▼▼▼▼▼▼

November

1 ....
2 ....
3 ....
4 ....
5 ....
6 ....
7 ....
8 ....
9 ....
10 ....
11 ....
12 ....
13 ....
14 ....
15 ....
16 ....
17 ....
18 ....
19 ....
20 ....
21 ....
22 ....
23 ....
24 ....
25 ....
26 ....
27 ....
28 ....
29 ....
30 ....

GRATITUDE
▼▼▼▼▼▼▼▼▼

December

1 ....
2 ....
3 ....
4 ....
5 ....
6 ....
7 ....
8 ....
9 ....
10 ....
11 ....
12 ....
13 ....
14 ....
15 ....
16 ....
17 ....
18 ....
19 ....
20 ....
21 ....
22 ....
23 ....
24 ....
25 ....
26 ....
27 ....
28 ....
29 ....
30 ....
31 ....

Photograph Credits

Photographs courtesy of Stocksy United: © Marija Kovac, page 49; © Sonja Lekovic, page 127; © Marcel, page 77; © Pixel Stories, page 45; © Melanie Riccardi, pages 98–99; © Helen Rushbrook, page 100; © Tatjana Zlatkovic, page 121.

Photographs courtesy of Shutterstock: © 5 second Studio, page 57; © Olha Afanasieva, page 15; © Kryvenok Anastasiia, page 87; © Art_man, page 23; © ArtMood, page 53; © AV_ photo, page 30; © Butterfly Hunter, page 72; © CK2 Connect Studio, page 19; © ddmirt, page 109; © Mari Dein, page 27; © graja, page 114; © Jen Huang, front and back cover; © Interpass, page 125; © Damir Khabirov, page 117; © LesiChkalll27, page 103; © LightField Studios, pages 10 and 12; © mama_mia, page 67; © Igisheva Maria, page 59; © Maria_lh, pages 2–3; © Ameena Matcha, page 81; © Smetana Natasha, page 63; © New Africa, pages 8–9 and 36; © Nyvit-art, page 94; © optimarc, page 46; © Ortis, page 104; © Alena Ozerova, pages 70 and 128–129; © PHENPHAYOM, pages 68–69; © Photographee.eu, page 40; © Vladimir Prusakov, page 84; © PV productions, pages 38–39; © TabitaZn, page 1; © Vereschagin, page 93; © vhpicstock, page 35; © Savanevich Viktar, pages 142–143; © Ann Volosevich, pages 4, 7, 11, 12, 14, 16, 18, 20, 22, 24, 26, 28, 30, 32, 34, 36, 41, 42, 44, 46, 48, 50, 52, 54, 56, 58, 60, 62, 64, 66, 71, 72, 74, 76, 78, 80, 82, 84, 86, 88, 90, 92, 94, 96, 101, 102, 104, 106, 108, 110, 112, 114, 116, 118, 120, 122, 124, 126, and 130–141.

Hardcover ISBN 978-0-593-23211-8

Design by Danielle Deschenes
Photograph credits appear on page 142.

Published in the United States by WaterBrook, an imprint of Random House, a division of Penguin Random House LLC.

Ink & Willow and its tree colophon are trademarks of Penguin Random House LLC.

Printed in China

2020—First Edition

10 9 8 7 6 5 4 3 2 1

Special Sales
Most WaterBrook and Ink & Willow books are available at special quantity discounts when purchased in bulk by corporations, organizations, and special-interest groups. Custom imprinting or excerpting can also be done to fit special needs. For information, please email specialmarketscms@penguinrandomhouse.com.